GOAT:
Women in Sports

T0191342

Serena Williams
≥ Tennis GOAT ≤

 Gareth Stevens
PUBLISHING

HOT TOPICS

BY KRISTEN RAJCZAK NELSON

Please visit our website, www.garethstevens.com. For a free color catalog of all our high-quality books, call toll free 1-800-542-2595 or fax 1-877-542-2596.

Library of Congress Cataloging-in-Publication Data
Names: Rajczak Nelson, Kristen, author.
Title: Serena Williams : tennis GOAT / Kristen Rajczak Nelson.
Other titles: Tennis greatest of all time
Description: Buffalo, New York : Gareth Stevens Publishing, [2025] |
    Series: GOAT : Women in sports | Includes bibliographical references and
    index.
Identifiers: LCCN 2023035486 | ISBN 9781538293775 (library binding) | ISBN
    9781538293768 (paperback) | ISBN 9781538293782 (ebook)
Subjects: LCSH: Williams, Serena, 1981–Juvenile literature. | African
    American women tennis players–Biography–Juvenile literature. | Women
    tennis players–United States–Biography–Juvenile literature. | Women
    Olympic athletes–United States–Biography–Juvenile literature. |
    Working mothers–United States–Biography–Juvenile literature.
Classification: LCC GV994.W55 R345 2025 | DDC 796.342092
    [B]–dc23/eng/20230828
LC record available at https://lccn.loc.gov/2023035486

First Edition

Published in 2025 by
Gareth Stevens Publishing
2544 Clinton St
Buffalo, NY 14224

Designer: Leslie Taylor
Editor: Kristen Rajczak Nelson

Photo credits: Cover (photo) Leonard Zhukovsky/Shutterstock.com, (wreath) Igoron_
vector_3D_render/Shutterstock.com, (banner, cover & series background) RETHELD
DESIGN IRI/Shutterstock.com, (tennis icon) RedlineVector/Shutterstockcom; pp. 5, 19
Jimmie48 Photography/Shutterstock.com; p. 7 Kingkongphoto & www.celebrity-photos.
com/https://commons.wikimedia.org/wiki/File:Venus_and_Serena_1993.jpg; p. 9
Paulobrad/https://commons.wikimedia.org/wiki/File:Serena_Williams_embraces_
Venus_Williams_as_Father_looks_on.jpg; p. 11 Paul Sutton-PCN/Alamy.com; p. 13
Neal Simpson/Alamy.com; p. 15 Everett Collection/Shutterstock.com; p. 17 photoyh/
Shutterstock.com; pp. 21, 23 lev radin/Shutterstock.com; p. 25 Joe Seer/Shutterstock.
com; p. 27 Dorothy Hong/Shutterstock.com; p. 29 Leonard Zhukovsky/Shutterstock.
com.

Printed in the United States of America

Some of the images in this book illustrate individuals who are models. The depictions do not imply actual situations or events.

CPSIA compliance information: Batch #CSGS25: For further information contact Gareth Stevens, New York, New York at 1-800-542-2595.

Find us on

Contents

Historic Athlete

Calling Serena Williams the tennis GOAT—greatest of all time—may not be enough. She's one of the greatest **athletes** of all time! From winning Olympic gold to besting her older sister to win titles, Serena's accomplishments are unmatched.

WHAT A STAR!

Serena's older sister Venus is also a tennis star. They have played doubles **matches** as a team as well as played against each other in singles matches!

5

Kids on the Court

Serena Jameka Williams was born September 26, 1981. She was raised with four older sisters in Compton, California. Serena's parents, Richard and Oracene, started teaching her and Venus tennis when they were young. Serena started playing around age 3.

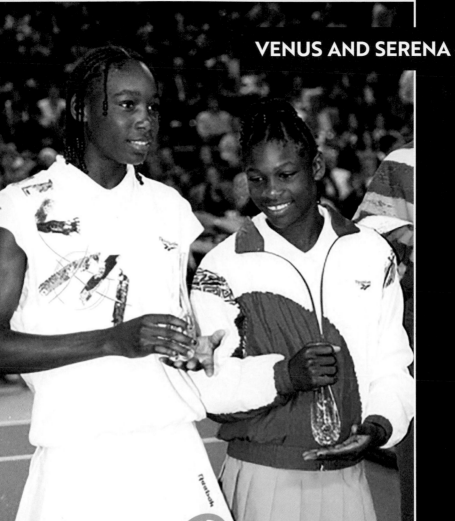

WHAT A STAR!

The family moved to Florida in 1991 so
Serena and Venus could go to a special
school for young tennis players.

Teenage Pro

At just 14 years old, Serena played in her first **professional** match. She lost. Her next pro match wasn't until 1997. But by the end of 1997, she **ranked** in the top 100 of women's tennis players in the world.

RICHARD WILLIAMS

WHAT A STAR!

Serena's dad, Richard, left his job and started coaching his daughters full time around 1995.

A Big Win

Serena played in her first Grand Slam, or major, **tournament** in 1998 at the Australian Open. Venus beat her in the second round. Then, in 1999, Serena won the U.S. Open! At almost 18, she was one of the youngest women ever to win a singles major.

1999 U.S. OPEN

WHAT A STAR!

Serena's first major wins were in 1998. She and Max Mirnyi won the Wimbledon and U.S. Open titles in mixed doubles, which is a tennis team with a man and a woman.

Double Up

Serena and Venus were also winning doubles titles together! They won titles at the French Open, U.S. Open, and Wimbledon in 1999 and 2000. It was no surprise when they won Olympic gold **medals** as a team in 2000!

WHAT A STAR!

The Williams sisters faced each other in singles matches often. In 2002, Serena beat her sister at three major tournaments!

At the Top

In 2002, Serena ranked number one in the world for 57 weeks straight! The following year, she won the Australian Open for the first time. This completed her **career** Grand Slam, which means she had won each of the four major tennis tournaments in her career.

Following a few seasons of being hurt on and off, Serena headed to the Olympics with Venus in 2008. They won gold in doubles again!

Golden Girl

Serena ranked number one again in 2009. She remained in or near the top 10 every year leading up to the 2012 Olympics. There she completed a career Golden Slam by winning a gold medal in singles! She and Venus won gold in doubles again too.

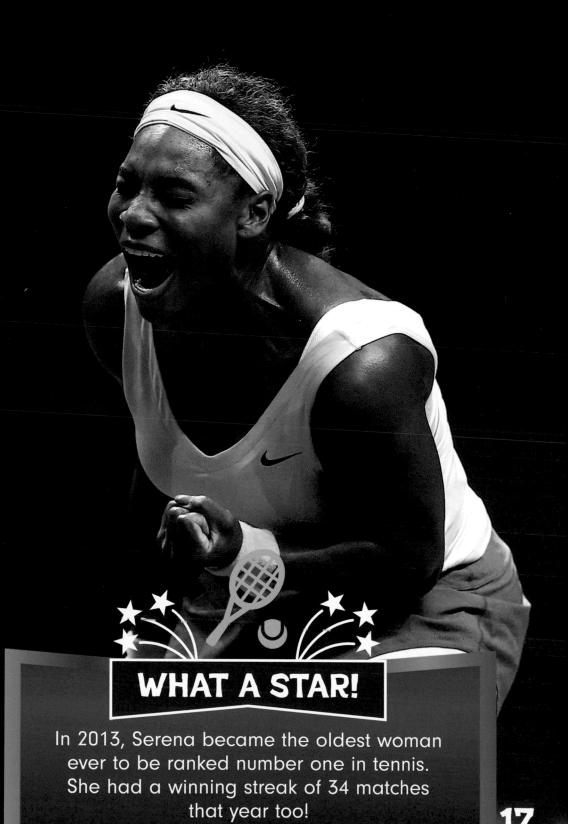

WHAT A STAR!

In 2013, Serena became the oldest woman ever to be ranked number one in tennis. She had a winning streak of 34 matches that year too!

Breaking a Record

Serena continued to be one of the best in the world. She ranked number one again in 2014 and 2015! In 2017, Serena beat Venus at the Australian Open. Serena had now won 23 Grand Slam tournament titles, a record in the **open era**.

WHAT A STAR!

Serena was named female athlete of the decade in 2019.

Family Time

Soon after, Serena took a break from tennis. She married her husband, Alexis Ohanian, and gave birth to their daughter, Olympia, in 2017. She started playing again in March 2018, but she didn't win an event again until 2020.

SERENA WITH HUSBAND ALEXIS OHANIAN

WHAT A STAR!

Serena was **pregnant** with Olympia when she won the Australian Open in 2017!

Retirement

Serena tried to fight her way back to the top of women's tennis. But she got hurt again in 2021 and couldn't get a major win in 2022. Serena announced that she would retire, or end her career, after the U.S. Open in September 2022.

WHAT A STAR!

Serena wrote in 2022: "I'd like to think that thanks to me, women athletes can be themselves ... They can wear what they want and say what they want and kick butt and be proud of it all."

Beyond Tennis

Serena became a star on the tennis court, and her accomplishments made her a star off it too. She has been part of making her own shoes, clothing, and jewelry lines. Today, she runs a company that helps women- and Black-owned businesses.

WHAT A STAR!

Serena is well known for wearing clothes that make a statement, on and off the tennis court!

25

Serena uses her fame and success to help others. She speaks out about what she believes in, including equal pay for women in sports. She traveled to Africa and, seeing a great need, was part of starting two schools in Kenya.

WHAT A STAR!

In 2003, Serena's oldest sister, Yetunde Price, was killed. The Williams family started a center named for her to help the Compton, California, community.

Greatest Ever

Serena's power on the court changed women's tennis forever. Her ability to stay on top for much of her long professional career makes her more than just a talented athlete. It makes her the GOAT!

WHAT A STAR!

Serena told *Sports Illustrated* in 2015:
"I do want to be known as the greatest ever."

Serena Williams
BY THE NUMBERS

Age in first professional match: 14

Age in last professional match: 40

Olympic gold medals: 4
(3 doubles, 1 single)

Grand Slam titles: 39
(23 in singles, 14 in doubles,
2 in mixed doubles)

Number one seasons: 5
(2002, 2009, 2013, 2014, 2015)

For More Information

BOOKS

Buckley, James. *Tennis Titan!: Serena Williams at Wimbledon in 2002*. Minneapolis, MN: Bearport Publishing, 2024.

Doeden, Matt. *Trailblazing Women in Tennis*. Chicago, IL: Norwood House Press, 2023.

WEBSITES

Serena Williams
www.wtatennis.com/players/230234/serena-williams
Follow all the latest news about Serena on the court!

Serena's World
www.serenawilliams.com
Check out everything about Serena on her website.

Glossary

athlete: Someone who is physically fit and takes part in sporting events.

career: The job someone chooses to do for a long time.

match: A contest between two athletes or teams. A women's tennis match is usually made up of three sets. Each set is usually made up of six games.

medal: A prize given to the winners of a competition. They are often made of metal and worn on a ribbon around the neck.

open era: During this time, beginning in 1968, all players, amateur or professional, could compete at the four Grand Slam events: the U.S. Open, the French Open, the Australian Open, and Wimbledon.

pregnant: Carrying a baby.

professional: Earning money from an activity that many people do for fun.

rank: To have a certain position in a group of athletes earned by winning or losing at a sport.

tournament: A series of contests testing the skill of many athletes in the same sport.

Index